NUMEROLOGY FOR KIDS

BY JENNY DEE & STEPHANIE FOLEY

Numerology for Kids

For Bradley & Luna
Numbers cannot count how big our love for you is!

Numbers...numbers....numbers! They are all around us and a very important part of our lives. Can you think of all the ways that we use numbers?

We can use them to count, number pages and create our own personal phone numbers. We use them in math to add, subtract, multiply, divide and more!

When some people grow up, they use numbers in their jobs, like scientists, business owners, cashiers, computer programmers, photographers and so many more.

Numbers can tell us how old we are, what date it is on the calendar and how hot or cold the weather is. They also help us to tell time.

In fact, there are so many ways to use numbers, it is hard to list them all!

How else do you use numbers?

In this book, we would like to show you one other very special way to work with numbers.

We are talking about "Numerology"(*noo-muh-**rol**-uh-jee*). Numerology is the belief that each number has a special meaning or energy. Think of it as each having its own unique personality, just like you and me.

Numerology was based on the study of number patterns and how they matched certain events or behaviors. In this book, we will talk about the basic numbers and some of their meanings, as well as how you can figure out some of your own personal life numbers that tell part of the story of who you are.

Get ready for a journey into the world of Numerology, explorers!

We will start with some ways that people use numerology to find out the numbers that are the most important in their lives. We have chosen to share just three kinds of personal numbers with you to get you started. There are so many more left to explore, but for this book, we will focus on the **Life Path, Expression** and **Heart's Desires** numbers.

Later on, we will review what each number means, as well as talk about some extra special numbers. Let's go!

Life Path Number

Our Life Path number tells us about the energy of who we are meant to be. It is like a clue into our "mission." How do you know what your special life path number is? Get ready to do some math, or have a grownup help you!

How to figure out your Life Path: First, you need to know the month, day and year you were born. Then, you add those numbers all together until you have a single digit. Let's pretend your birthday is November 13, 2007.

First, you add the numbers of your month. November is the 11th month of the year, so its number is 11, which has two digits. To get a single digit, we can add the two like this:
$11 = 1 + 1 = \mathbf{2}$

Then you add the day. $13 = 1 + 3 = \mathbf{4}$

Now it's time to add your year. $2007 = 2 + 0 + 0 + 7 = \mathbf{9}$.

Then add all three numbers together. $2 + 4 + 9 = \mathbf{15.}$

Since that total is still two numbers big, we need to break it down again until it is only one. $1 + 5 = \mathbf{6.}$

If this was your birthday, your Life Path number would be **6!**

Expression Number

Our Expression number can tell us a lot about our special talents, as well as our challenges in life. Some people also call this the Destiny number. It is based on the entire name you were born with—the one that your parents wrote on your birth certificate.

But how can you find out a number using letters? That is a great question!

Each letter of the alphabet has a number that represents it, just like a month does. In the same way that November is the 11th month of the year, the letter "B" is the 2nd letter of the alphabet, so that number is "2." The letter "Q" is the 17th letter of the alphabet. Since that is two numbers long, we have to add those together until it is only one number. $1 + 7 = 8$, so the letter "Q" would be an "8."

We created a chart on the next page to make it easy for you to figure out which number matches each letter. We also give you month numbers to help you with your Life Path number, too.

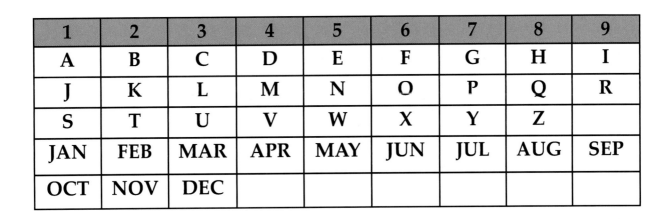

1	2	3	4	5	6	7	8	9
A	B	C	D	E	F	G	H	I
J	K	L	M	N	O	P	Q	R
S	T	U	V	W	X	Y	Z	
JAN	FEB	MAR	APR	MAY	JUN	JUL	AUG	SEP
OCT	NOV	DEC						

How to figure out your Expression: Using the chart above, add up the numbers of the letters of your full name. Include your middle name, too. Let's use this name as an example.

Joanna Lynn Doe

J(1) + O(6) + A (1) + N(5) + N(5) + A(1) + L(3) + Y(7) + N(5) + N(5) + D(4) + O(6) + E(5)

1 + 6 + 1 + 5 + 5 + 1 + 3 + 7 + 5 + 5 + 4 + 6 + 5 = 54

Since 54 is a double number, we need to add those numers together to get a single number. 5 + 4 = 9.

Joanna's Expression number is **9!**

Heart's Desire Number

This personal number tells us what we want in life. Some people also call this a Soul Urge number. Similar to your Expression number, it uses the letters of your name, but this time, it only counts the vowels (A, E, I, O and U).

The letter "Y" can be a little tricky here. If it acts like a vowel, like in "Mary," it counts as a vowel. But if it acts like a consonent, like in "Yasmin," you don't include it in your math.

How to figure out your Heart's Desire: Take your full name again, but only add up the vowels. Use the chart to help you find the right numbers for each vowel! Let's use Joanna as an example again. We underlined only the vowels.

Joanna Lynn Doe ("Y" acts as a vowel in "Lynn")

O(6) + A(1) + A(1) + Y(7) + O(6) + E(5)
6 + 1 + 1 + 7 + 6 + 5 = 26

Let's make this one number now. 2 + 6 = 8

Joanna's Heart's Desire number is **8!**

What Now?

We have learned how to figure out a life path, expression and heart's desire number using some pretend examples to help you find yours.

Now, you might be wondering what these numbers are all about. How can they tell you about your mission, your talents and challenges and what you want in life?

The next part of our book helps to explain what the numbers 1 to 9 represent in numerology. You will also see details about what each can tell you if it is your personal life path, expression or heart's desire number.

Let's find out what these numbers mean!

ORIGINAL ONE

General Meaning & Message: When you think about the number one, would it surprise you to learn that is all about one thing: you? That's right! It represents being original and unique. It also means leadership, courage and independence. When you see the number one, it is reminding you that you are strong and brave and that you can do anything you put your mind to.

If Your Life Path is 1: You are a natural leader with great ideas and the ability to follow your dreams. You encourage others to do their best by being a good example to follow.

If Your Expression Number is 1: You aren't afraid to follow your heart and make dreams come true. Since you are so good at doing things by yourself, being part of a team might be a struggle for you.

If Your Heart's Desire is 1: Whatever you love, you want to be the one in charge. Always remember that it is okay to be different because that's when you shine brightest!

TEAM PLAYER TWO

General Meaning & Message: The number two is about helping others. It represents working together, cooperating and being fair. When you see the number two, it might be telling you that someone needs your help or that you need to listen to someone else's side of the story and not just your own so you can get along better.

If Your Life Path is 2: You are natural at being a good member of a team. Since you are fair, you work well with others to accomplish a goal where everyone's ideas are heard.

If Your Expression Number is 2: You are very good at listening to and helping other people. People trust you! Although you can work well with a team, sometimes you put everyone else's needs and ideas before your own.

If Your Heart's Desire is 2: You love to feel like you belong, and people are important to you. You want everyone to get along! When you believe in yourself, you can make a difficult situation better by using your own voice and ideas.

THEATRICAL THREE

General Meaning & Message: Three is a number of joy, creativity and expressing yourself. It wants to laugh and play and make the world brighter! When you see the number three, it might be telling you to have more fun and do what you love.

If Your Life Path is 3: You are naturally creative, which also means you can be a great communicator or performer. You tend to be an optimist, which is someone who has a positive attitude in life.

If Your Expression Number is 3: You have a way with words and people are drawn to your enthusiasm. Sometimes you have so many exciting projects and activities going on, that you find it difficult to focus.

If Your Heart's Desire is 3: You have a great sense of humor and love to laugh, entertain and talk. Just remember that it is okay to share the sadder feelings, too, because life is about balance.

FOCUSED FOUR

General Meaning & Message: The number four is usually serious, responsible and loyal. It is all about keeping promises and working hard. If you happen to see the number four, it could be a message to be more responsible about something in your life. Four reminds you that you get rewarded for doing a good job!

If Your Life Path is 4: You are naturally a good worker and people look up to you and depend on you. You can build, organize and fix anything to make it work! Your magic is in planning and following that plan.

If Your Expression Number is 4: You are very good at coming up with great plans and solutions that help others. Although you are very organized, you might sometimes be a little stubborn about trying new things or ideas.

If Your Heart's Desire is 4: You like when things are in proper order and are more comfortable with a routine. It is important to remember that life does surprise us with changes, and sometimes you have to go with the flow.

16

FREEDOM FiVE

General Meaning & Message: Five is for freedom, adventure and being curious about the world around you. There is always something new to learn! When the number five comes around, maybe it is asking you to try something new or keep an open mind to other ideas.

If Your Life Path is 5: You are a natural explorer who loves to be free to follow your mind to learn and experience new things. You usually use your new knowledge to teach others or to help the world become a better place.

If Your Expression Number is 5: You love a good adventure! You are flexible and can adapt well to change because of your curious mind, but you might want to slow down sometimes and not rush through your experiences.

If Your Heart's Desire is 5: You love when you can explore, learn, travel or use your brilliant thinking skills. Although you can get bored easily, don't forget that you have to be responsible sometimes, too.

SWEET SIX

General Meaning & Message: Six represents caring for others, especially for family and the community. It is a little different than the number two, which is just being part of the team. Six takes the lead in serving others. Seeing a number six might be telling you that someone needs your love and compassion.

If Your Life Path is 6: You are a natural family person who wants to make sure everyone around you is happy and taken care of. You are very kind, generous and patient. You most likely are deeply artistic in some way.

If Your Expression Number is 6: You are a people person who is loving, loyal and affectionate. Even though you like to be there for others, it's important for you to also take good care of yourself.

If Your Heart's Desire is 6: Being with family and friends is very important to you. However, so is alone time. Your loved ones need time for themselves and so do you!

STUDIOUS SEVEN

General Meaning & Message: The number seven can be very mysterious. Like a detective, it likes to investigate, research and study all the facts and uncover secrets. If the number seven appears to you, it might be telling you that you are about to learn something new or discover a truth.

If Your Life Path is 7: You are a natural deep thinker who is interested in learning or challenging the world's wisdom, scientific theories and the unusual. It is common for people to find you trustworthy and honest.

If Your Expression Number is 7: You are someone who likes to analyze, research and investigate mysteries. Sometimes you get so involved with your mind, that you forget to include other people in your adventures.

If Your Heart's Desire is 7: You love to dig deep below the surface to discover the truth and figure out life's puzzles. It is okay to let your heart show you the way and not just your mind all the time.

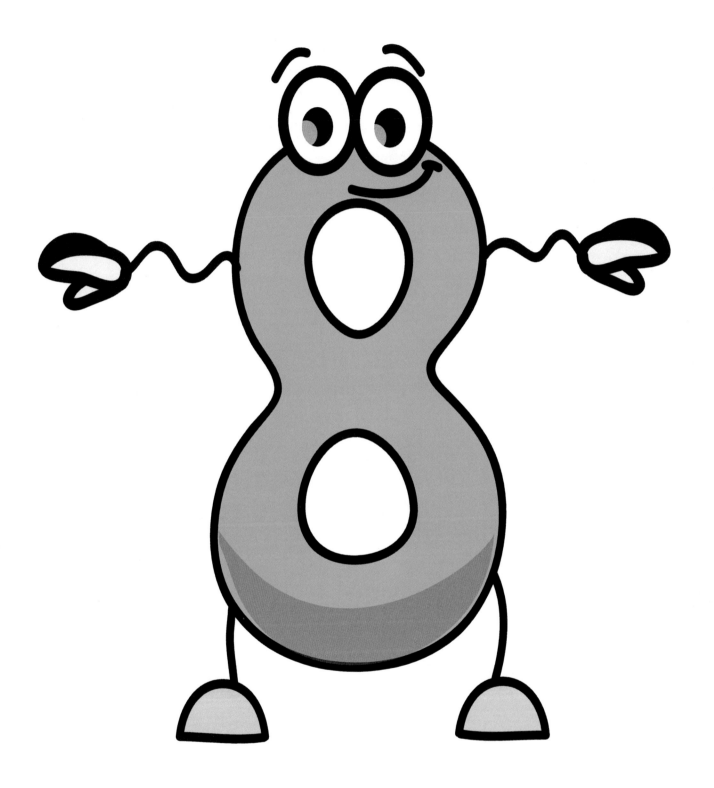

EXCELLENT EIGHT

General Meaning & Message: The number eight brings to mind the image of success. Think of this number as the energy behind your dreams, like taking action and working hard. Seeing the number eight might be a little message to you to not give up and to keep reaching for the stars!

If Your Life Path is 8: You are a natural success and know that you have the ability to achieve anything that you want in life. You are dedicated to your dreams and don't give up easily, which also makes you a great role model for others.

If Your Expression Number is 8: You have an excellent mind for business and reaching your goals. You really can do anything! Just remember that relationships with friends and family are just as special as your accomplishments.

If Your Heart's Desire is 8: You have big visions for a wonderful life, and that could mean success, money or power. Don't forget there is more to life than being important and having nice things.

NiCE NiNE

General Meaning & Message: The number nine is all about making the world a better place, from being charitable to fighting for the rights of others. Seeing the number nine could be telling you that there is something important that you can do to be of service to others less fortunate than you.

If Your Life Path is 9: You are naturally compassionate and giving, with a desire to generously give of your time, talents and possessions to help those who need it most. You are like a people magnet for being friendly, nice and entertaining.

If Your Expression Number is 9: You express yourself in a very artistic way and can understand other's emotions, which makes you able to help them better. Just don't get so involved in your own emotions that you forget about helping other people.

If Your Heart's Desire is 9: Your deepest wish is for the world to be at peace and for everyone to be happy and healthy. Be careful not to help others just for approval or fame. Do it because it is the right thing to do.

But What About Zero?

We have explored the meanings of 1 to 9, but what about 0, you might ask? Well, when using numerology with our birthdays or letters in our name, it is impossible for the numbers to add up to a zero. However, if you see a zero, this number also has a message for you!

Zero is at the beginning of all things, where nothing exists until there is something there, like the very first number, one. So, when you see a zero, it can be trying to tell you that something new is about to happen or that anything is possible because you are ready create something amazing.

Master Numbers

We showed you how in figuring out your life path, expression and heart's desires that you add up the numbers until they are only a single digit. However, there are a few two digit numbers that have a special meaning, such as 11, 22 and 33, because they double themselves. They are called "master" numbers.

If any of your personal numbers add up to an 11, 22 or 33, before you add them down to a single 2, 4 or 6, you have an extra special message waiting for you!

The master number 11 takes the meaning of its single number (2) and blasts it off into space! It wants to tell you that when you do something incredible, you become an inspiration for others, like a superhero!

The master number 22 is even stronger than its single number (4), and gives you an ability to build or create something spectacular, not just as a worker, but as a true leader who can bring a big vision to life.

The master number 33 takes the kindness of its single number (6) and allows you to share all of your knowledge and wisdom to give others hope and to help them learn from your own experiences.

Repeating Numbers

In addition to the three master numbers, other repeating numbers like 44, 55 and others are called power numbers because they make the energy of that number even stronger. Sometimes you might even see bigger repeating numbers, like channel 222 on the television, a $99.99 price tag or 33,333 miles on the car. Even those numbers have a message for you!

In fact, you might often see 11:11 on the clock, and some people think it is such a lucky number that they make a wish when they see it! All those powerful number ones are telling you to remember who you are and what you truly want in life.

As you can tell, numbers can be a unique way to learn more about yourself and even get reminders to think, behave or create in a certain way to make your life or the lives of others better.

Have some fun noticing the numbers that show up around you and see what messages they have for you!

AN IMPORTANT REMINDER

Numerology is not an exact science and can have many different interpretations based on what people believe. The ideas in these books belong to the authors, who are sharing their own beliefs based on many years of study and experience with different numerology experts, books and other fun resources. We hope that this book ignites a passion for you to explore your own beliefs about numbers! We want to give you some simple tools and ideas to get you started on your journey.

ABOUT THE AUTHORS

Jenny Dee

Jenny is an independent author, who loves to write anything from poetry and blogs to children's books and full length novels. It is her wish to take readers on an inspirational journey; one that will empower them to live with hope and courage. Jenny has studied astrology and numerology for over 10 years and always wished there was a way to teach her own two children about it in a simple way. She is so excited to share her soul school series books with the cosmic kids around the world, who find the magic of the universe as amazing as she does. You can find more of her books on her website: www.jennydeeauthor.com.

Stephanie Foley

Stephanie is a creative consultant who uses astrology, psychology, art and ancient and modern wisdom to help people navigate the creative process. She helps others read their own personal treasure maps so they can share their abilities with the world. Everyone has unique talents and treasures, which can be more easily identified using methods like astrology and numerology. She hopes the cosmic kids will learn about themselves and the gifts they can share with the world. You can find out more about her on her website: www.enchantedlife.me.

Subscribe for More Fun!

Interested in learning more? Scan our code to subscribe to our mailing list to receive sneak peaks into new books, upcoming events or special promotions!

Made in the USA
Middletown, DE
15 October 2020